A Beautiful Mess:

Light After Dark

By: M. Rene

Tiff Ann,

This one's for you

For all that you do

Without you by my side

I would not have survived

You helped me through my darkest times

DON'T GIVE UP

A Beautiful Mess

I'm learning to start loving me

Teaching myself to be more free

And I'm trying to stop being so depressed

I must confess

It's a beautiful mess

M. Rene

Drowning in sorrow

Waiting for tomorrow

Maybe it'll be better

Damn I wish I never met her

A Beautiful Mess

Our love was unraveling right before my eyes

There was no way to hide it

it could not be disguised

realizing its over

I feel so paralyzed

I'm crying on the bathroom floor

And you can hear my cries

You won't even come near me

And try to apologize

You've given up completely

Don't even want to try

There's nothing I can do

Our love has capsized

M. Rene

Everyone that came before you

Was nothing but a crashing wave

Knocking me down

One by one

Wave by wave

You were my soft wave

Gently lifting me up

Holding me close

My Deep Sea

A Beautiful Mess

All around me

I can see the wonders of the world

But I'm trapped behind the glass

Of my shattered soul

M. Rene

Inhale... Exhale... 123
These techniques aren't working
Can't you see?

Inhale... Exhale... 123
Everything's crashing around me
I can't breathe

Inhale... Exhale... 123
Please make it stop
I'm losing hope
With each teardrop

I can't go on
I'll be gone by dawn

Inhale... Exhale
123

A Beautiful Mess

As she wanders on and

Her colors wash away

The world begins to only

See her in black and grey

M. Rene

You fucked me up in the head

You won't hurt me

That's what you said

Before I met you

I thought I couldn't get worse

But now I'm laying in my tub

Fully submerged

A Beautiful Mess

She says

You need to let your guard down

And trust me

But how can I trust her

When my own mother left me

M. Rene

You read some of my poems today

Then asked me

If I was ok

A Beautiful Mess

I'ts 4 am

And I can't sleep

My anxiety is

Consuming me

Sometimes I feel too much

Sometimes I feel too little

There is never a

Happy medium

A Beautiful Mess

This one's for you

You know who you are

You broke me down

And gave me my scars

M. Rene

My father showed me how to be a good person

My mother showed me how not to be

-Daddy's Girl

A Beautiful Mess

It's ok

To not be ok

Your happiness will come

One day

M. Rene

Self-harm is an intense thing

It's like being stuck in between

Wanting to die

Yet yearning for life

A Beautiful Mess

The clock is ticking

Your time is now

So get up & start fixing

If you need help ask **how**

M. Rene

As a child when you fall

You cry and ask for help

When did we evolve into adults

Who fall silently

-Ask for Help

A Beautiful Mess

You left me alone

To fight life on my own

I could never figure out why

You left me high and dry

I needed you by my side

But all you cared about

Was getting high

M. Rene

I Am Not Ashamed;

A Beautiful Mess

Once someone cheats on you

You'll never be the same

Constantly questioning your worth

And thinking you're to blame

Letting your guard down

Will feel impossible

How can you trust again

When you have this gaping hole

M. Rene

I forgive you

For leaving me

But it still hurts

Everywhere I look you're all I see

Can't get you out of my brain

Just wish I could go back to being carefree

A Beautiful Mess

Find your happiness

And never let it go

M. Rene

Emotional abuse is just as

Damaging as physical

A Beautiful Mess

She told me

I'd amount to nothing

I'm gonna prove her wrong

By becoming something

M. Rene

You keep telling me

I deserve better

But I don't want better

I want you

A Beautiful Mess

I may be broken

But I'm not shattered

My pieces are just

Slightly scattered

M. Rene

I may be a wreck

But I'm not a disaster

My pieces will

Eventually be gathered

A Beautiful Mess

I would not have survived without you

I wish I could show you

If you only knew

You built me up

When I was broken down

Pulled me out of the water

I almost drowned

M. Rene

I've been depressed

Since I was 10

I've always wondered if it'd get better

And when

A Beautiful Mess

Looking in your eyes

I can see that

I am what you despise

What I don't understand

Is why

M. Rene

Moving on doesn't mean

You gave up

It just means you

Know your worth

A Beautiful Mess

The best thing I ever did

Was get over you

M. Rene

When you hurt

I hurt too

A Beautiful Mess

I'm proud of myself

Scars and all

I hurdled my demons

And broke down my walls

M. Rene

It wasn't easy

I still have my bad days

All that matters is I get up

And continue on life's maze

A Beautiful Mess

Unzip my heart

And uncover my soul

Beneath all this darkness

There's a beautiful girl

M. Rene

Please don't ever

Let me go my dear

For losing you

Is my biggest fear

A Beautiful Mess

Intertwine your soul with mine

And then maybe

Everything will be fine

M. Rene

You never deserved me

I knew this from the start

But that didn't stop me

From chasing your heart

A Beautiful Mess

You kicked me when I was down

Threw my ass right on the ground

But that is where I learned to grow

A blooming flower

Rising from my lows

M. Rene

In the past they may have fled

But I am here for what lies ahead

You never have to worry again

For I will be here till the end

A Beautiful Mess

I love you

Very much

But

Very much

Just ain't

Enough

M. Rene

These scars don't represent

Weakness

I had the strength to

Carry on

A Beautiful Mess

You ruined that girl

In every way possible

Her innocence and childhood

Will never be soluble

She lost all trust and faith

All because of your rape

M. Rene

She's had enough breakdowns

So be the one that sticks around

Don't be another let down

A Beautiful Mess

Be brave

With a kind heart

& don't let the world

Tear you apart

M. Rene

Look down at your feet

And you will see

Fragmented pieces of me

A Beautiful Mess

Our love will last infinity

This life

The next life

Eternity

M. Rene

Forever is not long enough

I'd need another day

And in that day

We'd plot a way

That we could run away

A Beautiful Mess

If our love was a movie

I'd watch it everyday

And when it would come to an end

I'd simply hit replay

Hold her tight

And let her know

It'll be alright

A Beautiful Mess

What if I miss you

Would that be ok

If I pulled in your driveway

What would you say

Would you open the door

And let me stay

Or simply push me away

M. Rene

Don't look at it as regression

Or you'll never see progression

Take them setbacks

And let them fall through the cracks

Take a deep breath

And relax

A Beautiful Mess

I was going through some shit

And you were too

But you pushed your shit aside

And focused on mine

M. Rene

I'm not gonna say it

For everyone to see

But I think you're a dog

If you know what I mean

A Beautiful Mess

There's a little chaos

In her soul

But that's what makes her

So beautiful

M. Rene

I was a wreck

Trying to be perfect

You said I was defect

And gave me nothing but neglect

You seemed surprised when I left

What did you expect

A Beautiful Mess

You can't just throw me away

I am not disposable

You promised me you'd stay

Are you just not capable

I wanted to give you the world

And show you every piece of me

But you wanted a different girl

So I'm left here picking up my heart's debris

M. Rene

Through all the chaos

And bullshit in the world

Spread kindness

A Beautiful Mess

She was broken

A hidden token

Lost in a cruel world

Dying on the inside

Looking for a bright side

M. Rene

I've spent my whole life

Trying to patch my broken past

But some things are not fixable

The pain will never pass

As days go on it'll get easier I'm sure

But there will never be

A definite cure

A Beautiful Mess

I'm tired of hiding

Behind this mask

Pretended I'm not affected

By my past

M. Rene

You have a broken soul like me

But you handle your pain differently

A Beautiful Mess

Take me somewhere and let's get lost

So I can forget all my thoughts

Just one day is all I ask

I just need a moment to forget my past

M. Rene

I've got a broken soul

And a heart with a

Gaping hole

A Beautiful Mess

We all have pain

It's time to make a change

Let's all come together

We can save each other

M. Rene

You're like a cigarette

An addiction I can't quit

I know that I should flee

Because you're slowly killing me

A Beautiful Mess

The world was oblivious

Of her breaking heart

Never taking her serious

And constantly tearing her apart

M. Rene

We're all living in

A cruel world

With damaged souls

A Beautiful Mess

I dreamed we'd live life happily

That was nothing but a fantasy

I didn't want to accept the reality

That you'd cause me nothing but agony

M. Rene

Unfortunately our love was a catastrophe

My heart being the casualty

A Beautiful Mess

I yearn for life that is

Simple and blissful

It is important to always

Stay wishful

M. Rene

Your silence is

Screaming at me and

I can feel it in the air

There's no way to fix this

Our love is beyond repair

A Beautiful Mess

She's a modern-day medusa

Venomous from the start

With a stone-cold heart

M. Rene

If I know that I can make a difference

Then maybe all this pain

Is worth it

A Beautiful Mess

I wont settle for half of you

Or even ninety-five percent

Give me your everything

Or nothing at all

M. Rene

My religion is kindness

And I will spread it

Until the day I die

A Beautiful Mess

What you see is not always what you get

Be careful who you choose

To spend your whole life with

M. Rene

They always say there's

Growth in pain

But this pain feels like

It's killing me

A Beautiful Mess

You are a beautiful soul

Who makes me feel whole

Your laugh and smile

Drive me wild

I'm loving your style

I hope you stay for while

M. Rene

Promises are sometimes left unspoken

Or even worse they are broken

But these are things I refuse to do

My promises were made for you

A Beautiful Mess

Don't do it

Hold on a little longer

I know you don't believe me now

But this will make you stronger

You can't stand it

Your head is full of monsters

Take a deep breath ask for help

These monsters can be conquered

M. Rene

Take care of yourself

Especially your mental health

A Beautiful Mess

You left me when I was three months old

I never had your hand to hold

You jabbed my heart with a knife

And now you want back in my life

I'm sorry mom but that door's closed

In fact the entire house is foreclosed

I will not hurt because of you anymore

You can keep trying but I will ignore

M. Rene

We settle for the ones

That hate us

And hate the ones

That love us

A Beautiful Mess

We have grown numb

Ignoring what the world's become

We can't ignore this any longer

Together we can make this world stronger

With love and kindness anything can be conquered

M. Rene

You will spend the rest of your life

Searching for me

In every person you meet and see

A Beautiful Mess

I only think of you once a day

The first second I'm awake

And then you never leave my brain

M. Rene

You were the poison

That I couldn't stop drinking

A Beautiful Mess

She wants to save me

But there's nothing

Left of me to save

In the first place

M. Rene

With you it's different

Than it's ever been before

You picked my broken body

Up off the cold hard floor

A Beautiful Mess

People change

I can't be mad at you for that

I just wish you leaving

Didn't hurt me so bad

M. Rene

We have that old time

Kind of love

Back when everything

Was black and grey

And love last a lifetime

A Beautiful Mess

I gave you the best me I could be

Along with my heart's key

Yet you still chose to flee

I guess it's true love has no guarantee

M. Rene

You moved on so fast

While I'm here with my heart smashed

What does she have that makes her better

You think she'll love you more

Never

A Beautiful Mess

We are living life in black and white

Avoiding people's basic human rights

Little kids are fighting for their life

Society only cares about if they're alright

Disregarding what other's are going through

Not taking time to look at others point of view

Change is way overdue

M. Rene

Some will tell you, you're not

But you **ARE** enough

So brush your knees off

And get back up

A Beautiful Mess

We are living in a world

Where shootings have become normality

That to me is complete insanity

M. Rene

Your scars will remind you that you survived

Always remember the reasons why

You were put on this earth to live not die

A Beautiful Mess

I went six months living each day

With a smile on my face

And each night

In a total mental craze

M. Rene

I know what it's like

To not want to live

So trust me when I say

You can get through this

A Beautiful Mess

We are at a dead end

There's nothing left to say

It's time to go our separate ways

M. Rene

The pain of being raped

Never fully subsides

It's one of those things

That never dies

And affects you the

Rest of your life

A Beautiful Mess

My high school art teacher

Taught me how to be a dreamer

And showed me I can use art as a healer

She was one of my first believers

M. Rene

I found an escape

Something that masked the pain

Every night I'd paint and paint

Until my fucking fingers ached

A Beautiful Mess

She cried for help every day

Waiting for someone to take the pain away

She just needs someone who will stay

And let her know it'll be ok

M. Rene

No matter what they say

You matter

Sometimes you may not feel that way

But give it time you will one day

A Beautiful Mess

Scars on her arms

Holes in her heart

But none of these things

Will tear her apart

M. Rene

I'm mentally exhausted

Been through all my options

My heart is full of toxins

It's time to take precautions

A Beautiful Mess

Shattered glass all on the floor

Don't want to do this anymore

There's a letter in my drawer

Just want to gain my wings and soar

Deep down in my heart's core

I know that I can fight this war

And be stronger than I ever have before

M. Rene

My doctor prescribed me this medicine

It's supposed to make me happy again

I just wanted to get rid of this pain

But now I'm going completely insane

A Beautiful Mess

Life's a battle

But you are a warrior

M. Rene

Even the blind can see

But we don't want to face reality

The problem in this world

Is our hearts are turning cold

If we open our eyes

And learn to empathize

As a whole we can rise

A Beautiful Mess

Everyone has their setbacks

What matters is how you react

Take life's struggles

And be humble

Save me from myself

For I'm not doing well

A Beautiful Mess

I'm better but I'm not healed

My heart still wears an iron shield

Protecting from love's battlefield

M. Rene

I just can't fight this feeling

That I'm meant for something great

Maybe all these life events

Really are my fate

I want to show the world

That life is what you make

And no matter what you feel inside

WE are NO mistake

A Beautiful Mess

I always thought

You weren't capable of loving

Turns out you just weren't capable of loving

Me

I was the problem

Now I

See

M. Rene

2AM and I'm still awake

Can't get rid

Of this heartache

A Beautiful Mess

You called me today

And I declined

I no longer care

I've mentally resigned

We used to have a love

So soft

So kind

But I'm moving on

And I'm leaving you behind

M. Rene

I hope you find peace

Prosperity

Whatever it is your heart seeks

Find it and be happy

Even if it is without me

A Beautiful Mess

When will I be freed

From this treachery?

M. Rene

It's comforting to know

There's others like me

Struggling in life

Trying to be happy

A Beautiful Mess

I'm stubborn and I overanalyze

But I will love you

Until the day I die

M. Rene

One day you were here

The next day you were gone

And I still don't understand

What I did wrong

A Beautiful Mess

I have everything I could ever want or
need

Yet this darkness still finds me

Maybe this is how

My life was meant to be

M. Rene

I'm a work of art

Abstract

My paint is bright and somewhat

Cracked

But still I'm a rare

Artifact

Who was born to make an

Impact

A Beautiful Mess

I write for the broken

Lonely and lost

The bruised and battered

Who are mentally exhaust

Please don't give up

Just keep on going

Even when you feel

Your whole world is closing

You are a strong fighter

Whose world WILL get brighter

You'll be freed and happy

Just hold on and you will see

M. Rene

;

Made in the USA
Middletown, DE
03 February 2019